20th Century
PERSPECTIVES

The United Nations

Stewart Ross

Heinemann Library
Chicago, Illinois

© 2003 Reed Educational & Professional Publishing
Published by Heinemann Library,
an imprint of Reed Educational & Professional Publishing,
Chicago, Illinois

Customer Service 888-454-2279

Visit our website at www.heinemannlibrary.com

Produced for Heinemann Library by Discovery Books
Designed by Ian Winton
Illustrated by Stefan Chabluk
Consultant: Robert Hudson
Picture research by Rachel Tisdale
Originated by Dot Gradations
Printed by Wing King Tong in Hong Kong

07 06 05 04 03
10 9 8 7 6 5 4 3 2 1

Library of Congress Cataloging-in-Publication Data
Ross, Stewart.
  The United Nations / Stewart Ross.
    p. cm. -- (20th-century perspectives)
Summary: Discusses the establishment of the United Nations, its function
in preventing war and eliminating poverty, and its role in various
international conflicts.
Includes bibliographical references and index.
  ISBN 1-40340-152-7
  1. United Nations--History--Juvenile literature. [1. United
Nations--History.] I. Title. II. Series.
  JZ4984.6 .R67 2003
  341.23--dc21
                            2002004550

Acknowledgments
The author and publishers are grateful to the following for permission to reproduce copyright material: p. 4 Corbis/Angelo Hornak; pp. 5, 15, 31, 33, 37, 40, 41, 42, 43 Popperfoto/Reuters; pp. 6, 14 Bettmann/ Corbis; pp. 7, 20 Hulton Getty; pp. 8, 9, 16, 23, 28, 29, 34, 35 Hulton Archive Photos; pp. 10, 19 Hulton Deutsch; pp. 12, 13 (Olivier Matthys), 21, 22, 24 (Eric Feferberg), 27 (Kanni Sahib) Popperfoto; p. 18 Corbis/Leif Skoogfors; p. 25 Corbis/David & Peter Turnley; pp. 26, 32 Corbis/ Howard Davies; pp. 30 (Mark Edwards), 36, 38 (Shehzad Noorani), 39 (Herbert Giradet) Still Pictures.

Cover photograph reproduced with permission of Hulton Getty. On the cover of this book, a UN tank driven by soldiers from Great Britain is shown escorting an aid shipment in the Balkans.

Every effort has been made to contact copyright holders of any material reproduced in this book. Any omissions will be rectified in subsequent printings if notice is given to the publisher.

Some words are shown in bold, **like this.** You can find out what they mean by looking in the glossary.

Contents

What Is the United Nations?

On the east side of Manhattan in New York City is a huge rectangular building overlooking the East River. Outside, bearing the emblems of almost two hundred nations, is a long, curved line of flagpoles. But even though the building is in New York City, it is not in U.S. territory. Instead, the building stands on an eighteen-acre (seven-hectare) international zone. It is the headquarters of the most daring experiment in global cooperation ever undertaken—the United Nations.

The international club

The United Nations, or UN, was founded in 1945 to promote world peace, to assist people in determining their own future, and to help develop social and economic well-being around the globe. It is not in any sense a world government. Instead, the UN is a meeting point, an organization that brings together just about all the independent nations of the world to help settle their differences and work together more closely.

The UN is like a club. The nations of the world join, pay a membership fee, and get what benefits they can out of being in the club. It is run by a permanent staff that manages its numerous branches. These branches specialize in matters such as international law, **humanitarian** aid, and peacekeeping. In the General Assembly of the UN, the voice of the smallest nation can be heard alongside the most powerful, each having an equal say.

The UN headquarters in New York. The tall building houses the UN's administration, while the General Assembly meets in the building on the right.

A checkered history

As we consider the global horrors that have occurred since the UN's founding, such as wars, massacres, famine, and fearful destruction of the environment, we may wonder whether the organization has achieved anything. Indeed, the UN has many critics who condemn it for discussing much but achieving little. However, as we will see, despite its many failures, the UN has chalked up many small but notable successes.

The history of the UN, therefore, is a mixed one. It was established to preserve peace, but it has spent more time trying to restore peace after fighting has broken out. It strives to eliminate poverty, but it has seen the gap between rich and poor nations grow ever wider. Would the world have been safer and fairer, though, if the UN had never been set up? Probably not, but the question cannot be answered for sure. The pages that follow will help you reach your own conclusion.

A UN peacekeeping soldier from Zambia gives water to Rwanda's Hutu refugees in 1995.

Purposes of the United Nations

The UN explained its purposes, as set out in its charter, as follows:
- *to maintain international peace and security*
- *to develop friendly relations among nations*
- *to cooperate internationally in solving international economic, social, cultural, and humanitarian problems and in promoting respect for human rights and fundamental freedoms*
- *to be a center for harmonizing the actions of nations in attaining these common ends*

The League of Nations

How can we prevent this from ever happening again? U.S. President Woodrow Wilson, (front center), a key figure behind the idea of the League of Nations, inspects war damage in France after the end of World War I.

People have long dreamed of creating a world in which peace and cooperation could replace war and conflict. In 1595, for example, the Duke of Sully, the French statesmen, suggested creating a world army to keep global peace. In the next century, the religious leader William Penn thought that the world would be at peace if everyone spoke the same language.

At the end of World War I in 1918, U.S. President Woodrow Wilson put forward a concrete plan for establishing an organization that would work to maintain world peace. The organization he proposed became known as the League of Nations.

Created in France by the Treaty of Versailles in 1919 and based in Geneva, Switzerland, the League of Nations was in some ways similar to the modern United Nations. It had an assembly, in which all member nations had a vote, and a council to keep the peace. Its large secretariat, or administrative department, undertook many **humanitarian** tasks, such as helping to settle the huge number of **refugees** created by World War I and by its peace settlements. Forty-two nations joined the League of Nations when it was formed.

President Wilson's dream

In January 1918, President Woodrow Wilson announced to Congress "Fourteen Points" to guide the postwar peacemakers. The last point sowed the seeds of the League of Nations. The United States never joined the League because the U.S. Senate would not allow it: *"A general association of nations must be formed under specific covenants [contracts] for the purpose of affording mutual guarantees of political independence and territorial integrity to great and small states alike."*

Troubles for the League

The League of Nations, however, was seriously flawed. One reason for this was that key nations did not join. The U.S. Senate did not wish to get involved in overseas affairs and voted to keep the U.S. out of the League. Germany did not join until 1926, and the **USSR** (Union of Soviet Socialist Republics, or Soviet Union) waited until 1934. Another reason the League failed was that it could only act by a **unanimous** vote against a nation that broke the peace.

One example that highlighted the League's weakness occurred in 1923. The Italian **dictator** Benito Mussolini invaded the Greek island of Corfu. The League protested but was unable to put enough pressure on Mussolini to make his troops withdraw. He did leave eventually, but only after Greece paid him a considerable amount. Force had triumphed and the League had failed.

The League's lack of power was further displayed in 1931 when Japan invaded the Chinese province of Manchuria, in 1935–36 when Mussolini invaded Abyssinia (Ethiopia), and in 1939 when **Nazi** Germany took over most of Czechoslovakia. On each occasion, the league was unable to protect these countries. By the outbreak of World War II in Europe in September 1939, the League of Nations was a disgraced institution that no one respected.

A New Beginning

The failure of the League of Nations did not cause Western leaders to give up the idea of working for peace. One important meeting that focused on peace occurred in 1941, before the United States had joined World War II. U.S. President Franklin D. Roosevelt met with British Prime Minister Winston Churchill on board the battleship *Prince of Wales*, which was moored off the coast of Newfoundland. The two statesmen planned for peace by drawing up a document known as the "Atlantic Charter," which was a declaration of the principles of international politics that would be put in place after the war.

Beyond the Atlantic Charter

The charter offered such principles as **free trade,** freely chosen governments, and **disarmament** of the countries whose aggression had led to World War II. It also suggested that an international security system be set up. The charter's principles were later adopted by the United Nations.

President Franklin Roosevelt (left front) and British Prime Minister Winston Churchill (right front) meet on board the battleship Prince of Wales *in the western Atlantic Ocean in 1941 to draw up the Atlantic Charter.*

On January 1, 1942, 26 countries, including the **USSR** and the United States, signed a Declaration of the United Nations. The name "United Nations" came from President Roosevelt. All those who signed the declaration accepted the principles of the Atlantic Charter. Then the three major **Allied powers**—the United States, the USSR, and the United Kingdom—began planning for a United Nations Organization. Meanwhile, separate discussions began about setting up an **International Monetary Fund** and **World Bank.**

Difficulties and discussions

The countries involved in planning the organization had trouble agreeing on what it should do and how it would best work. The USSR, for example, wanted each of its voting **republics** to have separate membership. Great Britain was worried that the UN would take away its overseas **colonies.** Another major problem was how votes were to be taken in the Security Council, the organization that would be responsible for preserving peace.

A meeting was held to discuss these issues in 1944 at Dumbarton Oaks, an estate in Washington, D.C. China was also represented there. Another meeting was held in the USSR in Yalta, a city on the Black Sea in the Ukraine, in 1945. On April 25, 1945, just as World War II was coming to an end, the United Nations Conference on International Organization gathered in San Francisco, California. Fifty nations were represented, including 9 European countries, 5 countries from the **British Commonwealth,** 3 from the **communist** USSR, 7 from the Middle East, 3 from Africa, 2 from East Asia, and 21 from North, South, and Central America. Poland was not represented at San Francisco but was later admitted as one of the 51 founding nations.

The UN is born

The goal of the conference was to produce a charter setting out the basic principles and organization of the new United Nations Organization. Discussions lasted for two months. On June 26, 1945, the UN Charter was ready for signing. It came into effect four months later on October 24, 1945.

Delegates from the major world powers—the United States, the USSR, the United Kingdom, France, and China—meet in in San Francisco to sign the Charter of the United Nations in 1945.

The UN Charter

Influenced by the words of the U.S. Constitution, the UN Charter begins with the following words: *"We the people of the United Nations determined to save succeeding generations from the scourge of war . . . and to reaffirm faith in fundamental **human rights,** in the dignity and worth of the human person, in the equal rights of men and women and of nations large and small, and . . . to unite our strength to maintain peace and security, and . . . to employ international machinery for the promotion of the economic and social advancement of all peoples, have resolved to combine our efforts to accomplish these aims. Accordingly, our representative Governments . . . have agreed to the present Charter of the United Nations and do hereby establish an international organization to be known as the United Nations."*

A World Parliament

The central body of the United Nations, and the only one to which all members belong, is the General Assembly. It is a sort of world parliament that discusses a wide variety of issues, from terrorism to child labor. The General Assembly meets once a year, between September and December, but it can be summoned for extra sessions in times of crisis.

The General Assembly first gathered in London. However, after wealthy American businessman John D. Rockefeller, Jr., donated $8.5 million toward buying a site in New York, it was decided that the headquarters should be built there. This decision was controversial. Many felt that the UN should be based in a neutral country such as Switzerland, where the League of Nations had its headquarters.

UN membership

More controversy arose as founding members considered which countries, or "states" as UN member countries are called, should be UN members. With the United States and the **USSR** locked in a Cold War, neither **superpower** was prepared to allow its enemy's friends and allies into the UN. They finally

The opening session of the UN General Assembly in September 1979. The assembly is the only place where all nations, rich and poor, large and small, sit together as equals.

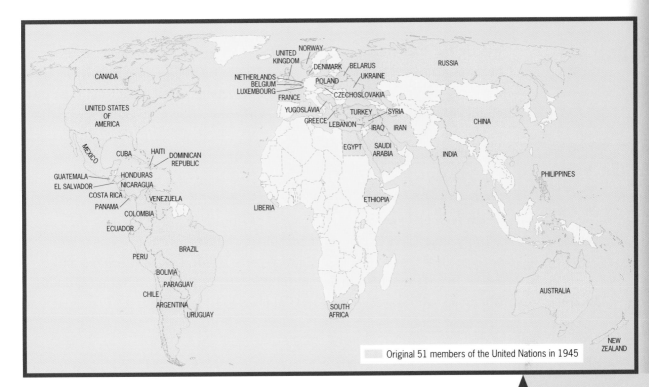

	Original 51 members of the United Nations in 1945

reached a compromise in 1955. Sixteen new countries were admitted. In the compromise, the U.S. agreed to the membership of **communist** Hungary and Romania, while the USSR accepted the membership of U.S. allies Spain and Ireland. Fifty new members were admitted between 1956 and 1968, many of them newly independent nations in Africa. A similar wave of new members came with the breakup of the USSR in the early 1990s. Vietnam and Germany were reduced to single representation when North and South Vietnam were united in 1977 and West and East Germany were reunited in 1990.

Language and meetings
The Assembly Hall at the UN is equipped with headphones members can use to listen to speeches, either in the language of the speaker or in a different language. Interpreters are stationed in the hall and translate speeches into the official UN languages—English, Chinese, French, Arabic, Russian, and Spanish.

The Trusteeship Council
The UN Charter set up the Trusteeship Council to look after eleven territories put under the protection of the UN in 1945. These territories, such as the Trust Territory of the Pacific Islands, which was formerly under the control of Japan, had belonged to powers defeated in World War II. In 1994, the Trusteeship Council was suspended when the last Trust territory, Palau (in the Pacific Ocean), became independent.

The founding members of the United Nations. By 1957 most of the remaining countries of Europe and southeast Asia had also joined. As African states gained independence from 1955 to 1977, they too became UN members. In 1991–92, the UN expanded to include former Soviet republics in the Baltic and central Asia.

Struggling Secretaries

The United Nations is run by its secretariat, an administration that by the beginning of the 21st century employed almost 9,000 people from 170 countries. They swear loyalty to the UN, rejecting special pleas from their own or any other country.

An impossible job?

The secretariat is headed by the secretary-general, who holds one of the most prestigious posts in world politics. U.S. President Franklin Roosevelt hoped the secretary-general would become a sort of global watchdog, alerting the Security Council to trouble and advising it what to do. However, it soon became clear that the best a secretary-general can do is to **mediate** and advise. In a statement confirming the difficulty of the position, Austrian Kurt Waldheim, who was secretary-general from 1972 to 1981, once described it as "the most impossible job in the world."

The first secretary-general was Trygve Lie from Norway. He did his best to make his post one of real power and influence. In 1949, when Mao Zedong's **communists** took over the government of mainland China, the ousted pro-**Western** government of Chiang Kai-shek fled to Taiwan. With U.S. backing, Chiang's government kept China's seat in the UN. Lie tried to get Chinese representation transferred to Mao's government but was prevented by the U.S., which condemned him for "taking sides" in the Chinese conflict.

Sweden's Dag Hammarskjöld was the second secretary-general of the UN from 1953 to his death in 1961. He is considered to be the founding father of UN peacekeeping. Here he visits UN peacekeeping troops in the Congo in 1960.

In 1950, Lie supported the Security Council's resolution for member states to provide aid for South Korea after it had been invaded by the communist country of North Korea. This time, the **USSR,** North Korea's ally, accused Lie of taking sides. In 1951, the Soviet Union **vetoed** Lie's reappointment. Lie resigned in 1952.

Personal priorities

During the era of the Cold War, similar difficulties were experienced by the secretary-generals who came after Lie. In 1967, for example, the United States accused U Thant of Burma, who served from 1961 to 1971, of yielding to pressure from Egypt's President Gamal Abdel Nasser. Thant had removed the UN peacekeeping force from Sinai, the peninsula in northeastern Egypt that borders Israel. In fact, Thant had no other choice. The presence of the UN force required the agreement of the host country, Egypt. Other secretary-generals had similar problems.

The end of the Cold War in 1990 freed the secretary-general from the need to balance the United States and the USSR but did not actually give the UN leader a great deal of freedom. For example, when Egypt's Boutros Boutros-Ghali, who was secretary-general from 1992 to 1996, tried to take a more active, independent line on international affairs, the U.S. government objected. Understandably, in April 2001, the reforming secretary-general Kofi Annan of Ghana decided to avoid political involvement and made a campaign to tackle the HIV/AIDS epidemic his "personal priority."

Secretary-General Kofi Annan from Ghana took office in 1997. He worked hard to improve the way the UN was managed and run. Annon's second term was renewed to 2006.

The secretary-general and the media

Secretary-General Boutros Boutros-Ghali struggled to prevent the U.S. media from exerting too much control over the UN. Addressing the U.S. press in 1995, he explained:

*"We say we have sixteen members in the Security Council: the fifteen members plus **CNN**. Long-term work doesn't interest you [the media] because the span of attention of the public is limited. Out of twenty peacekeeping operations, you are interested in one or two . . . And because of the limelight on one or two, I am not able to obtain the soldiers or the money or the attention for the seventeen other operations."*

International Law and Justice

World justice? The opening of the Court of International Justice took place in The Hague, Netherlands, in 1946. International justice is a good concept, but who decides what international law is and who sees that the court's decisions are carried out?

The United Nations manages one permanent court, the International Court of Justice, or World Court. The International Court of Justice started as the Permanent Court of **Arbitration,** which was established in The Hague, Netherlands, in 1899 to hear international disputes. After working with the League of Nations, the court became part of the UN in 1946.

The World Court

The World Court hears disputes between member states, offering a judgment that all parties have agreed to accept. The court can also give an opinion if an individual state or a branch of the UN, such as the Security Council, requests that it does.

Unfortunately, fewer than half of UN members have been willing to accept the court's judgments. Moreover, most states are unwilling to bring political matters before the court. This is partly because the international law that the court interprets is uncertain and disputed. So, while the World Court performs worthwhile tasks, its decisions have not been widely publicized.

Criminal courts

The same cannot be said of the UN's two criminal **tribunals** and its plans for a permanent international criminal court. In 1953, following the trials of **Nazi** and Japanese war criminals, the General Assembly called for the establishment of an international court to try people accused of **genocide.** The years passed, however, and nothing was done.

In the early 1990s, plans for an international criminal court were revived. Two events led the UN into action: genocide in Bosnia and Herzegovina, part of the former Yugoslavia, in the early 1990s and in Rwanda in central Africa. In Rwanda, hundreds of thousands of Tutsi people were massacred by the rival Hutus in a civil war in 1994. In 1993, the UN established the International Criminal Tribunal for Yugoslavia. The tribunal made world headlines in 2001 when Yugoslavia's former president, Slobodan Milosevic, appeared before it, charged with committing **crimes against humanity.** In 1994, an International Criminal Tribunal for Rwanda was established to try Rwandan leaders accused of genocide. The tribunal continues to try those cases.

Ex-president of Yugoslavia Slobodan Milosevic appeared before the UN's War Crimes Tribunal in The Hague, Netherlands, in 2001. In his defense, he claimed that the court was illegal.

Following popular acceptance of these two tribunals, the representatives of 160 UN nations agreed in 1998 to create a permanent International Criminal Court at The Hague. The court would try crimes such as "genocide, war crimes, and crimes against humanity." Secretary-General Kofi Annan hailed the move as "a giant step forward in the march towards universal **human rights** and the rule of law."

Against war criminals

The International Criminal Tribunal for Rwanda has the power to prosecute suspects accused of the following crimes against civilians:
a. murder
b. extermination
c. enslavement
d. deportation
e. imprisonment
f. torture
g. rape
h. persecutions on political, racial, and religious grounds
i. other inhumane acts.

The Security Council

Many of the United Nation's more exciting moments take place in the Security Council. The Security Council is the body that the UN Charter made responsible for international peace and security, and most important decisions are made by the Council.

The Security Council was originally made up of eleven members, five of them permanent—the United States, the **USSR,** the United Kingdom, France, and China. Six members were temporary and served for two years. This arrangement was revised in 1965, when the number of temporary members rose to ten. The number of temporary members was raised to give a more balanced geographical representation in the Security Council. In the 1990s, negotiations began for Germany and Japan to become additional permanent members of the Security Council.

The UN Security Council is shown in session in January 1946. Because the permanent members of the council could veto any decision, the council rarely took a decisive action for years.

The use of force

A major weakness of the League of Nations was its inability to back up its resolutions with armed force. The UN hoped to avoid this problem, and its Security Council was set up to be able to call upon a permanent force provided by member nations.

From the outset, the United States and the USSR could not agree on this force. The Soviets wanted twelve **infantry divisions,** for example, while the United States wanted twenty. In the end, there was no agreement. Consequently, whenever the UN needs armed forces, they are provided for a specific mission only by willing member nations.

Two phases

The history of the Security Council—and indeed, of the entire UN—since 1945 can be divided into two distinct parts. Until 1990, the Security Council was made powerless by a clause in the UN Charter that gave any one of the Council's five permanent members a **veto** over all major decisions. This was officially known as the "Great Power Unanimity Rule." From 1945 to 1990, the two great powers of the world, the United States and the USSR, were also enemies, and each used its veto to stop actions that could be beneficial to the other. In 1990, however, the USSR collapsed, and the Cold War ended.

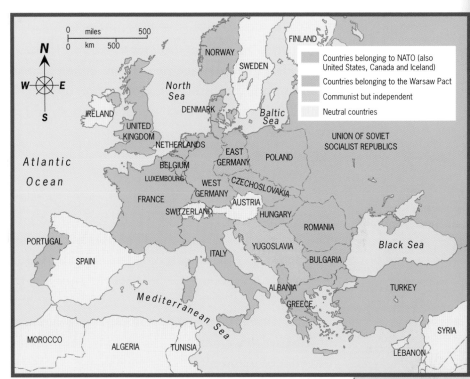

Russia emerged as a **democratic**-capitalist state, and it looked as if the Security Council might be able to work as it had been originally intended to in 1945.

Europe at the time of the Cold War (1947–90). The continent was divided between communism (mostly the Warsaw Pact countries) and capitalist democracy (mostly the members of NATO).

The Cold War

The United States and the USSR fought as uneasy allies in World War II. From 1946 on, fed by mutual misunderstanding and fear, relations between the two superpowers worsened. They never went to war, but they did fuel limited wars between other countries. This period of frightening global tension, which lasted until 1990, is known as the "Cold War." The United States and its allies formed a military alliance, the North Atlantic Treaty Organization (NATO). The USSR and its **communist** supporters were members of an opposing military and economic alliance, the Warsaw Pact.

Working for Peace

The first purpose of the United Nations, as stated in its charter, is "to maintain international peace and security." This is a massive and, some say, impossible task. Nevertheless, it is an important one, and the UN is the only organization in the world equipped to undertake it.

The maintenance of peace and security falls under two main headings, general and specific. The general includes the reason for the very existence of the UN—to bring people together to discuss their problems. It also involves **disarmament** and arms limitation, action to get rid of many of the causes of conflict such as poverty and lack of education, and spreading a general acceptance of basic **human rights.**

Peacekeeping measures

The UN Charter describes specific actions to be taken to maintain peace and gives powers to do this mainly to the Security Council. The 1945 San Francisco conference came up with a scale of peacekeeping measures. They range from the **pacific,** such as investigating tense situations, to the **coercive,** such as sending UN troops into the field against a country that attacks another.

Not long after peacekeeping measures were in place, the UN was using **arbitrators** to work out peace. In 1947, they headed to the Middle East to help control unrest after the establishment of the state of Israel, and in 1948 they were sent to the Indian state of Kashmir to maintain peace there. In the 1950s, Secretary-General Dag Hammarskjöld introduced a peacekeeping role for the UN. It involved sending in neutral UN troops, with the agreement of both sides in a conflict to keep warring factions apart. It also called for the United States and the **USSR** to agree to this. These forces were effective in a variety of war zones, from the Congo to Cyprus.

UN soldiers of UNPROFOR (UN Protection Force for Former Yugoslavia), wearing their distinctive blue helmets, shown in Bosnia in 1995. The UN was criticized for not being prepared to use sufficient force to keep the peace.

Intervention?

The charter prevented the UN from intervening in the internal affairs of any state. But this raised a difficult question—what about groups within a country that claimed to be independent but were not recognized as such by the country's governing power?

When situations such as these arose, the Security Council remained true to its charter most of the time. It refused to be drawn into conflicts in Northern Ireland, which was part of the United Kingdom from 1968 on, and in Chechnya, which was part of the **Russian Federation** from 1994 on. But the council did play an active role in Bosnia and the other newly independent states that emerged after Yugoslavia broke up in 1991.

The best and the worst

Secretary-General Kofi Annan offered this eloquent defense of UN peacekeeping:

"The first United Nations peacekeeping operation [Congo, 1960] was an attempt to confront and defeat the worst in man with the best in man: to counter violence with tolerance, might with moderation, and war with peace. Since then, day after day, year after year, UN peacekeepers have been meeting the threat and reality of conflict, without losing faith, without giving in, without giving up."

This Indian solider was a member of a UNEF that entered Egypt in 1956. This was the UN's first true peacekeeping (as opposed to observation) force.

Uniting for peace

According to the UN Charter, the General Assembly may "discuss any questions relating to the maintenance of international peace and security" and make recommendations to the Security Council or member states. In 1950, the Assembly went further than this with a "Uniting for Peace" resolution. This allowed it to take over the Security Council's role, even calling for UN troops, if a **veto** prevented the council from acting. The resolution was used several times during the 1950s, such as when the Assembly called for a United Nations Emergency Force (UNEF) for Suez in 1956. Invading British and French troops, aided by Israel, opposed the Egyptian government's **nationalization** of the Suez Canal.

Enforcement

Sometimes the United Nations approves the use of force to see that its decisions are enforced. Because the UN has no army or military commanders of its own, these enforcement actions are not under direct UN control. Instead, they are undertaken by certain countries with UN approval. In 1999, for example, a force led by Australia and supported by troops from 21 other member states entered East Timor, which is on an island in the Indian Ocean. Their task was to restore law and order after violence had erupted between East Timorese people seeking independence (with UN backing) from Indonesia and Indonesian forces unwilling to recognize East Timor's independence. Another example was the Gulf War against Iraq in 1991, which was led and largely conducted by the United States. After 1990, the UN also undertook enforcement on a smaller scale, involving only a few hundred troops, such as in Somalia from 1992 to 1995 and in Bosnia and Herzegovina from 1992 to 1995.

Bypassing the veto

An enforcement action in the name of the UN was undertaken in the Korean War, which took place from 1950 to 1953. At the end of World War II, Korea was liberated from Japanese occupation by two armies—Soviets troops in the north and American troops in the south. Korea was consequently split between a Soviet-backed north and a U.S.-backed south. In 1949 both forces withdrew. A year later, **communist** North Korea, equipped with Soviet arms, launched a surprise attack on the South.

U.S. forces fighting in the name of the UN, land at Inchon, North Korean, in September 1950.

The United States immediately sent troops to the South. At the same time, it called on the Security Council to authorize UN action against the North Korean aggressors. Normally the **USSR** would have **vetoed** any Security Council decision to intervene. On this occasion, however, the Soviets were **boycotting** the UN. They had withdrawn in

protest at Taiwan being the Chinese UN representative instead of the
People's Republic of China.

In the absence of the Soviet delegation, a resolution recommending member states to take action against North Korea was approved. This was the only time that the UN approved major enforcement action during the Cold War.

The Korean War

Although the United States provided the bulk of foreign troops in South Korea, sixteen other nations, including the United Kingdom, Australia, New Zealand, and Turkey, also sent troops. At first, the South Koreans and their allies were driven back to the southeast of the Korean peninsula. They then counterattacked and advanced all the way to the border with communist China in the north. At this point, the Chinese intervened and pushed the South Koreans back to the border between North and South Korea. Here the fighting became bogged down, until eventually it ended in July 1953.

American troops, fighting for the UN, resist an assault of Chinese troops during the Korean War. The war was the only time during the Cold War when forces went into battle in the name of the UN.

Korea remained divided. The North had lost perhaps a million men. China lost about 500,000, South Korea 600,000, and the UN 57,000, of whom 54,000 were Americans. While the League of Nations was never able to organize powerful countries to take action against aggression, the UN had shown that it could defy aggression by approving superpower action. The USSR made sure in the future that it was always represented at Security Council meetings.

The Blue Helmets

Between 1948 and 2002, the United Nations launched 54 peacekeeping operations, 41 of them after 1990. Although the Security Council sets up and plans peacekeeping missions, the secretary-general is responsible for managing and directing them. More than 120 states make military and civilian personnel available, and even Switzerland, one of the few countries that is not a member of the UN, provides money and equipment.

These statistics are impressive. Nevertheless, particularly before 1990, the blue-helmeted UN peacekeepers were rarely involved in actual combat. When they did become involved in fighting, such as in the Congo, the result was usually disastrous. Learning from that experience, later peacekeeping operations generally avoided involvement in conflicts and consequently were more successful.

Congo

One of the first UN peacekeeping forces, the United Nations Operation in the Congo, or ONUC, entered the newly independent **Republic** of Congo (later Zaire, now Democratic Republic of Congo) in 1960. It came after the Congolese prime minister, with the backing of the Security Council, requested that the force try to restore peace after civil war followed the country gaining independence from Belgium.

Hardly had ONUC become active when it found itself at the center of a political storm. It was resented by many Congolese, and even UN Secretary-General Hammarskjöld said **Western** nations were using the force to do "their dirty work in Congo." By this, he meant that he believed UN forces were supporting Western (especially Belgian) businesses, such as mining operations, in Congo. The **USSR** also believed that the UN was protecting Western interests, and it refused to pay for the mission. ONUC withdrew in 1964, and the fighting continued until the victory of rebel leader Joseph Désiré Mobutu in 1965.

In this photo, UN troops are shown waiting to board a plane going to the Congo in about 1961.

Cyprus

In 1964 the Security Council sent the United Nations Peacekeeping Force in Cyprus, or UNFICYP, to the Mediterranean island of Cyprus. Its assignment was to keep the peace between the minority Muslim Turks and the majority Christian Greeks. However, when Turkish forces invaded in 1974 to protect the Turkish minority and seized the northern part of the island, UNFICYP did little to resist them. The island remains divided to this day, with UNFICYP troops still patrolling its frontier.

El Salvador

When an eleven-year civil war ended in 1992 in El Salvador, a country in Central America, a UN force named the Observer Mission in El Salvador entered the country. Its task was to see that the cease-fire agreement between the **right-wing** government and its **left-wing** opponents held up. It was also assigned to make sure that various reforms, including greater rights for women and minority racial groups, land distribution, and help for the poor, were carried out and that free and fair elections were held. Three years later, the mission had successfully fulfilled its tasks and was disbanded.

A Canadian UN observer, shown in Cyprus in 1964. When the Turks invaded the island ten years later, the UN troops offered little resistance.

Modern failure

The end of the Cold War and the new spirit of cooperation that this brought to the Security Council did not mean that all UN peacekeeping missions were successful. In 1993, for instance, the United Nations Operation in Somalia II force was sent to Somalia, an east African country torn by civil war and famine. The UN force was instructed "to take appropriate action, including enforcement measures, to establish throughout Somalia a secure environment for **humanitarian** assistance." The force was met with fierce armed resistance, and in 1994 it was told to cease military action. It was withdrawn a year later.

The Gulf War

Many hoped that the end of the Cold War would bring a period of peace. Without two **superpowers** to support opposing sides, it was anticipated that conflicts would be more easily resolved. Moreover, freed from the Security Council **veto,** the United Nations would be able to make the world a safer place. The UN's actions in the Gulf War seemed to support such hopes.

Following Iraq's invasion of Kuwait in August 1990, UN Secretary-General Pérez de Cuéllar (left), who held the post from 1982 to 1992, talks with Iraqi minister Tarek Aziz.

Invasion of Kuwait

In 1990 Iraq's President Saddam Hussein accused his small but oil-rich neighbor Kuwait of drilling diagonally into Iraqi oil fields. He also claimed Kuwait was producing too much oil, forcing down the price. Iraq owed Kuwait billions of dollars it had borrowed to finance its war with Iran and was now being asked to pay up. Saddam decided to take action.

Iraq invaded Kuwait on August 2 and formally **annexed** Kuwait a few days later. Government leaders in the **West** had previously supported Saddam Hussein. Now, they were now worried that he would move from Kuwait into neighboring Saudi Arabia, the world's leading oil producer.

UN action

The government of the **USSR** was breaking up at this time, and its diplomats did not oppose the West's views. Because of this, the United States and its allies had little trouble persuading the Security Council to back action against Iraq. **Economic sanctions** were applied. When these produced no response, a resolution approving the use of "all necessary means" was agreed. It was not necessarily a formal call for force. Nevertheless, the United States and its allies interpreted it as supporting military action.

A multinational force, largely made up of U.S. military personnel, was assembled in Saudi Arabia. Military operations, code-named "Desert Storm," began in January 1991 with a six-week bombing campaign. Troops operating in the name of the UN crossed into Kuwait on February 24. Four days later, a cease-fire was called. Kuwait had been liberated.

A new era?

From the UN point of view, the Gulf War military actions were a success. Against Iraq's losses of some 110,000 soldiers and 10,000 civilians, the UN troops and allies had lost only 343 military personnel. Kuwait had been freed, Iraqi aggression had been put down, and collective security in which nations pooled resources to combat aggression was shown to work. A bright new era in UN history seemed to be dawning.

In the Gulf War, troops took aggressive action in the name of the UN for the first time since the Korean War 40 years earlier.

Others were less optimistic. They pointed out that Desert Storm's success had depended not on collective security but on the West's determination to protect its supply of cheap oil. They argued that if Saddam had moved against another neighbor—Iran, Syria, or Jordan, for example—the allies would almost certainly not have reacted so strongly. Furthermore, the Security Council's backing had depended more on the USSR's weakness than on its support. In other words, the circumstances of the Gulf War were quite similar to those of the Korean War.

Disarmament and Arms Limitation

Beginning in the nineteenth century, developers of weapons began to apply modern technology to their designs, making weapons more accurate, more powerful, and therefore more deadly. This created problems. Not only were the new weapons extremely destructive—they were also very expensive to make. Out of this situation, the modern **disarmament** movement was born.

The movement had a slow start. Individual nations approved arms limitation treaties, but more widespread disarmament was difficult to achieve. International disarmament conferences were held in 1899, 1907, and, under the League of Nations, in 1932–34. All failed to reach a common agreement.

Old cause, old difficulties

After the first use of **nuclear weapons** at the end of World War II, the United Nations took up the arms control cause. Article 11 of the Charter empowered the General Assembly to investigate the matter, and Article 26 asked the Security Council to construct "a system for the regulation of armaments."

With this as a goal, a Disarmament Commission was founded in 1952. The city of Geneva, Switzerland, hosted UN disarmament negotiations from 1962 to 1978. Meanwhile, various UN armament agreements were drawn up. In 1963 an agreement banning nuclear weapons testing was settled. An agreement banning **weapons of mass destruction** on the ocean bottom was created in 1970, and another banning the manufacture and use of chemical weapons was agreed to in 1993.

But the UN-sponsored efforts had little real effect, and the problems continued as before. Governments feared that large-scale disarmament would destroy their important armament industries, which would result in bankrupting many and making millions unemployed. Smaller-scale arms reduction would have similar but less catastrophic consequences.

Governments that dreamed of conquest or feared attack were also unwilling to disarm. Even if they agreed, they argued, who would make the first move, and who would monitor the process? The same arguments applied to arms reduction. A good example of the sort of problems the UN encountered came in 1946. The UN wanted nuclear weapons reduced in number or even eliminated entirely. The United States agreed, but said it would destroy its weapons only after an international system of weapons control was agreed. The **USSR,** which at that time did not possess nuclear weapons but was working hard to develop them, said the destruction of nuclear warheads should come before agreement on a system of control. This disagreement resulted in a deadlock, and the nuclear threat continued.

The UN found itself in the same position on this issue as it had been before. The organization had no independent power. Ultimately, the UN could do only what its members agreed to do. Its chief role was to **mediate** and encourage. Even when it oversaw the production of a **convention** or **treaty,** it could not guarantee that nations would endorse it. An example is the 1968 Treaty on the Non-**Proliferation** of Nuclear Weapons in which the United States, the Soviet Union, and the United Kingdom agreed not to help other countries develop nuclear weapons. France and China, both major nuclear powers, did not sign the treaty until 1992.

The head of the UN weapons inspection team discusses his work with an Iraqi official. The UN team's job was to find and destroy Iraq's weapons of mass destruction. The team was harassed by Iraq and withdrew in 1998.

The UN and Iraq
After the Gulf War, the Security Council banned Iraq from making or holding weapons of mass destruction and set up the United Nations Monitoring, Verification, and Inspection Commission to oversee the destruction of such weapons in Iraq. The UN also imposed measures that allowed Iraq to sell only enough oil to support Iraq's people. Saddam Hussein claimed the sanctions caused unnecessary suffering, and he continually hampered the commission's work. It was replaced by another commission in 1999. Ten years after the Gulf War, the UN and Iraq were no nearer to resolving their differences.

Closing the Economic Gap

The United Nations was never intended to be simply a peace-preserving organization. Its 1945 charter provided it with an Economic and Social Council (ECOSOC), whose function was to coordinate and supervise the UN's economic and social work. As the UN's peacekeeping and disarmament role ran into difficulties, its economic and social role expanded. As a result, by the end of the 20th century, ECOSOC had to use up about 85 percent of the UN budget, and its work was touching many times more lives than the Security Council's.

Expanding role

When ECOSOC was founded in 1945, it had just eighteen members, elected by the General Assembly for three-year memberships. Fifty years later, the membership had risen to 54, representing more than a quarter of all UN member countries. The reason for this increase is the huge variety of work undertaken by ECOSOC, ranging from tackling the problem of illegal drugs to monitoring the status of women worldwide.

UNICEF (United Nations International Children's Emergency Fund) provides free food and drink for the people of Vienna, Austria, in April 1948.

The council, which divides its time between New York and Geneva, supervises nine commissions, including the Commission on Crime Prevention and Criminal Justice and the Commission on Human Rights. It also oversees five Regional Commissions, including the Economic and Social Commission for West Asia, and works with a vast number of other UN committees, organizations, programs, and agencies. These include the United Nations International Children's Emergency Fund (UNICEF), the World Health Organization (WHO), and the sometimes controversial United Nations Educational, Scientific, and Cultural Organization (UNESCO).

UNICEF

The United Nations International Children's Emergency Fund (UNICEF) was created in 1946 to help European children after World War II. It became permanent in 1953. UNICEF works with governments, charities, and other organizations to help children all over the world. Its particular concerns are promoting education, health, and well-being for all children, regardless of gender, religion, or race. It wants all children to live in dignity and security. UNICEF is particularly famous for its greetings cards, which it sells to raise funds for its many projects.

The Commission on Sustainable Development

The Commission on Sustainable Development (CSD) was founded in 1992 and has been one of ECOSOC's successes. After the 1992 Earth Summit in Rio de Janeiro, Brazil, the CSD was charged with monitoring the progress of agreements made at the summit and advising on a wide range of environmental issues. Its overall aim was to produce a plan during the 21st century for world economic development that did not harm the environment. As concern for the environment grew, so did interest in the CSD's work. Its meetings attracted more than 50 government ministers and delegations from hundreds of other organizations around the world.

UNESCO

Secretary-General U Thant, speaking in 1968, said of the ECOSOC network that "for the first time in history, [it] provided mankind with mechanisms that would seek to improve the life of every man, woman, and child on earth." However, such work inevitably becomes wrapped up with politics and therefore highly controversial. This is the case with UNESCO.

In 1945, the United States had perhaps been UNESCO's most eager supporter. The U.S. believed the organization would promote peace through education and understanding. However, by the 1970s, UNESCO had come under the control of people who others considered to be **Third World radicals.** UNESCO's leaders claimed that all news and information was distorted because it all came from **Western**-owned media organizations.

In this 1949 photograph, children in Haiti write on a blackboard provided by UNESCO.

UNESCO's anti-Western political statements, inefficiency, and **corruption** infuriated the United States, which provided a quarter of the organization's budget. When UNESCO's director-general, Amadou-Mahtar M'Bow of Senegal, refused to reform, the United States left UNESCO in 1984. A year later, the United Kingdom followed. Some of the advisors to Ronald Reagan, the U.S. president at the time, even recommended that the United States leave the UN altogether.

World Health

As more advances were made in modern medicine, governments and charitable organizations tried to find ways to make its benefits available to everyone, especially those who couldn't afford to buy the medicine. Wealthier nations realized, too, that it was in their self-interest to stamp out disease in less-developed parts of the world to prevent it from spreading. With this in mind, the International Office of Public Health was set up in Paris in 1907, and the League of Nations Health Organization was established in 1923. In 1948 the work of these two organizations was absorbed into a new UN agency, the World Health Organization (WHO).

WHO at work

The goal of the WHO was much broader than that of its predecessors. While it was primarily concerned with disease control, the WHO aimed at "the highest possible level of health" for everyone. In other words, its program worked toward positive mental, physical, and social health and well-being, not just the absence of sickness. Behind this thinking was the belief that poor health, like poverty, was the cause of much of the world's discontent and conflict.

The WHO launched its most ambitious campaign, "Health for All by 2000," at the end of the 1970s. It was, perhaps, an impossible dream. Certainly the health of the human race was better at the end of the 20th century than it had been 30 years before, but some 25 percent of the world's people still suffered from treatable illnesses. Moreover, no sooner had one illness been brought under control than another appeared. The most obvious example of a recent and deadly sickness is acquired immune deficiency syndrome, or AIDS. The WHO also drew attention to obesity, the state of being very overweight, by collecting and publishing information on the problem.

Information, epidemics, and advice

Much of the work of the WHO involves collecting and passing on information about health-related matters. This means collecting statistics about the number of people suffering from malaria, for example, and keeping nations informed of the latest advances in cancer research.

WHO workers measure children in the Ivory Coast to discover the correct drug dosage needed to protect them from the disease onchoceriasis (river blindness).

A second area of WHO work involves fighting **epidemic** diseases. This is done by funding and organizing vaccination programs, educating national public health authorities, and making improvements to the environment, such as providing pure and safe water supplies.

The UN and AIDS

In many of its programs, the WHO works alongside other agencies. AIDS, for example, is too large a problem to be tackled by a single organization of the UN. The Joint United Nations Program on HIV/AIDS (UNAIDS) linked the WHO with UNICEF, UNDP (the United Nations Development Program), UNESCO, the World Bank, and other agencies. Together they conduct research, collect information, and advise how the AIDS epidemic may be controlled. Equally important, they also raise awareness about AIDS with information campaigns and by running the annual World AIDS Day.

Finally, the WHO spends much time and money helping to construct effective health services in UN member states. The work involves training, advising, funding, and assisting in every way possible so that one day each nation will be able to care adequately for the health of all its people.

Emergency!

Long before World War II ended, the **Allied powers** realized that when the guns finally fell silent, homes would have to be found for millions of **refugees,** and reconstruction would have to be started in the countries that were devastated by war. Therefore, two years before the United Nations itself was founded, the United Nations Relief and Rehabilitation Administration (UNRRA) was formed. Its main goal was to help the millions of refugees in Europe and Asia.

Refugees

In 1947 the UN replaced the UNRRA with the International Refugee Organization (IRO). This lasted only four years before it became the United Nations High Commission for Refugees (UNHCR), which began operating on January 1, 1951. Over the second half of the twentieth century, UNHCR helped an estimated 50 million people. Many, such as the Palestinians, Rwandans, and Afghans, became refugees because of war. Others, such as the Ethiopians and other Africans living on the fringes of the Sahara Desert, were driven from their homes by famine and drought. Whatever the cause, UNHCR provided refugees with basic necessities like food and shelter and then did what it could to enable them to return home.

UN soldiers help Cambodians return home in 1992. Many thousands had fled abroad to escape the bloodshed of the 1970s and 1980s.

Getting it together

When disaster strikes, whether it is an earthquake, a flood, or a war, there is usually an adequate supply of relief workers, goods, and money. The governments of developed countries have all developed emergency relief programs. Worldwide charities such the Red Cross, Oxfam, and the Red Crescent also step in to help during disasters. The UN also has its own agencies, such as UNHCR, the World Food Program, UNICEF, WHO, and others. But getting all these groups to work together is difficult and can cause problems. During the famine in Ethiopia in the mid-1980s, there were widespread reports of wastage, inefficiency, and **corruption.**

The UN is the obvious body to coordinate major relief operations because it has universal approval. However, it was not effective at coordinating such operations until 1997, when it established the Office for the Coordination of Humanitarian Affairs (OCHR). By 2000, OCHR was raising $1.4 billion to help 35 million distressed people in 16 separate countries and regions.

World Food Program

Plans for a World Food Program (WFP) that would send emergency food supplies to where they were most needed were drawn up in 1962. The program was to operate on a three-year trial basis, starting in January 1963. Before the end of 1962, however, there was an earthquake in Iran, a hurricane in Thailand, and the resettlement of five million refugees in Algeria. In all three locations, people were starving. The WFP started to work before its official launch date and has not stopped since.

Longer term

Natural disasters cannot be prevented. Nevertheless, steps can be taken to lessen their effect. So, as well as supplying immediate aid to those affected, the United Nations concentrates huge resources on helping societies recover and become less vulnerable to disasters that might happen in the future. This is the prime function of the United Nations Development Program (UNDP). The UNDP is concerned with promoting **democratic** government, as well as crisis prevention and recovery.

UN trucks arrive at the Mukaruka camp in Zaire (now called the Democratic Republic of Congo) to return Rwandan refugees to their homes. They had fled because of bloodshed in their own country in 1994.

Human Rights

Eleanor Roosevelt, wife of U.S. President Franklin Roosevelt, campaigned tirelessly for human rights. She was the chairperson of the UN Commission on Human Rights from 1947–51.

Since at least the seventeenth century, there has been talk of all human beings having basic rights. It was difficult to find agreement on what those rights were, however, and even more difficult to get governments and other authorities to respect them. The total lack of respect for **human rights** shown by several governments in the mid-20th century, such as the persecution of Jews in **Nazi** Germany and of the followers of certain religions in the **USSR,** prompted pioneers in the United Nations to take action.

The Universal Declaration

The UN Charter of 1945 spoke of human rights, and three years later these rights were defined in a Universal Declaration of Human Rights, adopted by the General Assembly on December 10, 1948. All member countries were urged to allow the text to be displayed and read in schools and in other educational institutions.

The declaration demands "universal respect for and observance of a common standard of achievement for all peoples." This is easier said than done. For example, Article Two of the declaration says the rights applied equally to everyone, no matter what their "race, color, sex, language, religion, political or other opinion, national or social origin, property, birth or other status." Yet some religious groups believe that women are inferior to men, while others believe certain social groups, or castes, are lower in social status than others. Some gender and social-rights issues also clearly conflict with religious rights.

Rights and reality

A UN Commission on Human Rights (UNCHR), established in 1946, produced several committees and declarations on rights-related subjects such as racism, women's rights, apartheid, the treatment of prisoners, and slavery. In 1993, the post of UN High Commissioner for Human Rights was created to

give the human-rights movement a sharper focus. Four years later, the post was given to retiring president of Ireland, Mary Robinson.

Even when headed by someone as well-known as Mary Robinson, the effectiveness of the UNCHR was limited. However, the Commission could put pressure on poor countries by threatening to withdraw UN aid unless certain human-rights violations were stopped. But the UNCHR could do little to persuade the governments of wealthy countries, such as oil-rich Saudi Arabia, to extend human rights to their citizens.

South African police in the African republic of Durban in 1959 attack black women who had been involved in a protest against apartheid.

Apartheid and South Africa

Apartheid means "separate development." It applies to the system established in South Africa after World War II that allowed for unfair treatment of people of different races. White people in South Africa were considered a "privileged minority," and other races were deprived of basic human rights. The UNCHR campaigned vigorously against apartheid. It did not get the support it might have hoped for from the **West** because South Africa was a powerful **anticommunist** force in southern Africa. This changed with the collapse of communism. By 1990, the West no longer needed the support of South Africa's all-white government, and apartheid was swiftly overturned.

The Rights of Women

When the United Nations was founded, discussion about **human rights** centered on issues such as fair trials, the right to vote, and freedom of speech. By the 1960s, however, the central rights issue had become race—specifically, outlawing racial prejudice. During the 1980s, the focus changed again. The new rights issue was the right of women to be treated equally with men.

New cause, new organizations

In the 1980s and 1990s, the UN set up a vast range of women's groups. At the center were the UN Division for the Advancement of Women (UNDAW), the UN Development Fund for Women (UNIFEM), and the International Research and the Training Institute for the Advancement of Women (INSTRAW). The call to address women's rights was also taken up by existing UN organizations, such as UNICEF, UNESCO, and WHO, all of which started giving priority to women's issues.

In Bangladesh, a group of women protest for women's rights on International Women's Day, a day organized by the United Nations.

The theme was also taken up by the Human Rights Commissioner, Mary Robinson, who declared in 1998, "There can be no human rights without women's rights." The UN organized world conferences on women. Special funds were set aside in developing countries specifically for women to start their own enterprises. At the same time, a huge amount of information on gender discrimination was made available in an attempt to get people and governments into action. One fact that the information showed was that of the 400 cases of domestic violence reported in the Punjab, Pakistan, in 1993, almost half resulted in the death of the wife.

Successes and failures

As with many causes taken up by the United Nations, there was much discussion but little specific action. All those who signed the first UN Charter were men. More than 50 years later, in 2001, the charter still bore the signatures of only four women, from the Dominican Republic,

the United States, Brazil, and China. Women were still second-class citizens in many countries. Few women held high positions in government or commerce, and forced marriage and brutality were widespread. Statistics showed that domestic violence was increasing, although this might have been because it was being reported more often.

Despite this gloomy outlook, progress was made, thanks in large part to UN pressure. In 1991, Mexico changed its rape law to help women victims. Turkey, traditionally a male-dominated society, established a Ministry of State for Women. Brazil set up special police units to deal with women's issues. Of course, changing customs that are thousands of years old takes more than a decade. Nevertheless, by the 21st century, the outlook for millions of women was certainly brighter than it had been twenty years earlier.

A huge dove of peace floats above the delegates to the UN's fourth World Conference on Women, held in Beijing, China, in 1995.

Advancing Women's Rights

From the Declaration of the UN Conference on Women, held in Beijing, China on September 15, 1995:

"We, the Governments participating in the Fourth World Conference on Women . . . Recognize that the status of women has advanced in some important respects in the past decade but that . . . major obstacles remain . . . [and] Dedicate ourselves unreservedly to addressing these constraints and obstacles and thus enhancing further the advancement and empowerment of women all over the world."

The Environment

The United Nations has faced two forces that threatened global destruction. One was nuclear war, which dominated the first 25 years of the United Nation's existence. By the late twentieth century, this threat had lessened and been replaced by something more complex but equally worrying—environmental catastrophe.

The gathering disaster

By the mid-1980s, reports were warning that human activity was seriously damaging the earth's environment. Gases from refrigerators and aerosols were destroying the **ozone** layer in the upper atmosphere that protected Earth from the sun's harmful rays. Industrial and domestic waste was polluting rivers, seas, and oceans. Millions of square miles of irreplaceable rain forest had disappeared.

Most alarming of all, the burning of fossil fuels such as oil, coal, and gas was surrounding the earth with a layer of heavy gases. These acted like the glass of a greenhouse, trapping the heat from the sun in the atmosphere. This "greenhouse effect" was causing global warming. The measurable rise in temperatures led to marked climate changes, expanding desert regions, and melting polar ice caps, causing sea levels to rise. Widespread flooding was predicted.

Global warming caused by pollution of the atmosphere is said to have been partly responsible for an increase in natural disasters. This severe flooding took place in Bangladesh in 1998.

The ozone layer—a UN success story

By the mid-1980s, it was clear that the earth's protective ozone layer was being depleted. In response, the UN Environmental Program brought together all industrialized nations in 1987 to agree to the Montreal Protocol. This phased out the production and use of gases that harmed the ozone layer by 1996, saving millions from contracting potentially lethal skin cancer.

Enter the UN

Because environmental change is a truly global problem, the UN is the best organization equipped to deal with it. However, as with its other work, it can act only with the permission and support of its members. Here, the UN runs into a

major difficulty. The United States is both the largest contributor to UN funds and the major source of "greenhouse" pollution. Its automotive industry, a large-scale polluter, is a huge employer. As a result, the UN faces perhaps the most serious danger in its history without the support of its richest and most powerful member.

The Earth Summit

Although it established an Environment Program (UNEP) in 1972, the United Nations did not recognize the seriousness of the environmental situation until 1983, when it launched a World Commission on Environment and

Development. The commission reported back to the General Assembly in 1987. What was needed, the commission said, was a worldwide conference on the environment.

The UN Conference on Environment and Development (UNCED)—the "Earth Summit"—finally met in Rio de Janeiro, Brazil, in 1992. Altogether, 178 governments were represented. After much talk, the Earth Summit produced a series of splendid-sounding declarations. However, since the conference attendees could not agree on how to enforce the declarations, they were destined to remain largely expressions of goodwill.

U.S. Vice President Al Gore addresses the Rio de Janeiro Earth Summit in 1992. Summit members were criticized by some for talking too much and doing too little.

Sustainable development

From the Rio Declaration on Environment and Development, 1992: ". . . human beings are at the center of concerns for **sustainable development.** They are entitled to a healthy and productive life in harmony with nature . . . States have a sovereign right to exploit their own resources but not to cause damage to the environment of other States."

Kyoto

By the time the nations of the world gathered again to discuss the environment, it was clear that the Rio Earth Summit had resulted in few concrete improvements. In 1997 another Earth Summit was held in Kyoto, Japan. Its goal was to find a way of making the 1992 United Nations Framework Convention on Climate Change (UNFCCC) work.

Three sides

The negotiating nations at Kyoto fell broadly into three groups. The majority belonged to developing nations that caused relatively little pollution and did not want strict controls over their future industrial expansion. A second group, largely European, was made up of the industrialized nations that were prepared to make the changes necessary to reduce the production of "greenhouse gases."

The third group included the United States, Australia, and, to a lesser extent, the **Russian Federation** and Ukraine. They were suspicious about the suggested levels of greenhouse gas reduction. Instead, they questioned the reality of global warming and suggested using large areas of forest to absorb extra carbon dioxide (a greenhouse gas).

The Kyoto Protocol

The negotiations were long and difficult, but eventually a **protocol** was drawn up. Developed countries pledged that between 2008–2012, they would reduce their overall average greenhouse gas output to seven percent below the 1990 levels. Politicians hailed the agreement as a victory for common sense.

Environmentalists, however, saw it as no victory at all. Many scientists had suggested that a cut of more than 50 percent was needed. Although the Kyoto Protocol was legally binding, there was no mechanism to bring defaulters to court. Besides, how could one bring a country to court if it refused to sign the protocol? The United States, for example, pulled out of the agreement in 2001.

Trade in emission quotas

The Kyoto Protocol accepted the U.S. government's idea of nations "trading" emissions. This allowed countries or companies to buy permission to emit pollutants. The seller was a country that had cut pollution more than it was required to do. The trading meant that a wealthy nation or business could buy its way out of meeting its Kyoto undertaking.

Different situation, same problem

The Kyoto Protocol highlighted the strengths and weaknesses of the UN. It had identified a serious global problem, assembled the nations of the world to discuss it, and presented them with a viable plan. In the end, though, it could do nothing to enforce the plan. It could do only what its members, particularly its more powerful members, would agree to.

The threat of **nuclear weapons** could be ended by destroying the weapons. Destruction of the environment could not be dealt with so simply. By the 21st century, it had become the UN's most difficult test. If it succeeded, future generations would owe the United Nations an everlasting debt.

After much discussion, delegates attending this 1997 UN-organized conference on climate change in Kyoto, Japan, agreed a treaty to halt climate change. Five years later, many countries had still not put the treaty into effect.

Protest!

Many Americans disagreed with their government's attitude toward the Kyoto Protocol. In 2001, the environmental group Save Our Environment asked its followers to send a letter to President George W. Bush that included the following words: *"I strongly oppose your decision not to regulate carbon dioxide emissions from the nation's power plants, and to pull the United States out of the Kyoto Protocol . . . Rather than rely on sound science and cost-effective solutions to the nation's environmental and energy needs, you have chosen to bolster fossil fuel interests that pollute our air and water and contribute further to global warming."*

Past and Future

The United Nations has reflected the world, not molded it. Any hopes that it would do otherwise were soon dashed in the tensions that led to the Cold War. Therefore, any criticism of the UN and its shortcomings is in part a criticism of the nations of the world.

The UN has been mocked for talking too much and doing too little and for passing resolutions but not seeing them carried out. Its procedures and methods have been criticized as inefficient, wasteful, politically biased toward poorer nations, and out of touch with reality.

Developing nations say the UN does too little to help them, while **Western** nations complain that they pay the most but receive the least. Critics also indicate that really important political decisions, such as arms reduction or peace enforcement, are made not by the UN but by individual states acting on their own initiative. Although set up to preserve world peace, the UN itself has not stopped a single conflict.

Successes

Most agree that the world would have been a poorer and more dangerous place had the UN not existed. Although it cannot force states to act, at least the UN brings them together and starts them talking. Had it not called for the Earth Summit and established the Kyoto Protocol, for example, a global environmental program would have been almost unimaginable.

The blue beret stands for peace, unity, and hope. UN soldiers and Rwandan refugee children are shown here in 1994.

The UN's most valuable work is carried out by its least glamorous agencies. Countless people are helped by its development program and its **human rights** campaigns. The **World Bank** and the World Health Organization also do invaluable work as part of the United Nations.

Reform and the future

In 1997 Secretary-General Kofi Annan launched UN reform that some agreed was long overdue. Measures

International terrorism—an old challenge returns. Damage to the Pentagon building in Washington, D.C., was caused when a hijacked airliner was flown into it on September 11, 2001.

included establishing the post of deputy secretary-general, streamlining administration, cutting administrative costs, and improving information distribution activities better to explain the UN's work. The changes were widely welcomed, especially by the United States, which had led criticism of UN wastefulness and bias. The UN emerged leaner and fitter.

It needed to be. As if peacekeeping and tackling environmental problems and poverty were not enough, after September 11, 2001, the United Nations faced yet another challenge: global terrorism. Its Security Council responded quickly to the terrorism, condemning the acts and calling for swift punishment for those responsible. The council also reaffirmed the need to combat any threats to international peace and security.

September 11, 2001

A week after the terrorist attacks on New York and Washington, D.C., the UN General Assembly (which had been evacuated on September 11) passed a resolution that included the following two clauses: *"The General Assembly . . .*

• *strongly condemns the heinous acts of terrorism, which have caused enormous loss of human life, destruction, and damage in the cities of New York, host city of the United Nations, and Washington, D.C. . . .*

• *urgently calls for international cooperation to prevent and eradicate acts of terrorism, and stresses that those responsible for aiding, supporting, or harboring the perpetrators, organizers, and sponsors of such acts will be held accountable."*

Timeline

1919	League of Nations formed
1923	Corfu Incident shows League of Nations' weakness as a peacekeeper
1939	Outbreak of World War II in Europe (to 1945)
1941	Atlantic Charter suggests the idea of a United Nations
1944	Dumbarton Oaks meeting sets out blueprint of UN
1945	UN founded in San Francisco
	UNESCO established
1946	General Assembly (51 members) first meets in London
	Security Council first meets in London
	Trygve Lie becomes first secretary-general of the UN
	East versus **West;** Cold War begins
	Court of International Justice set up
	UN moves to New York
1948	UN mission to Palestine
	World Health Organization established
	General Assembly accepts Universal Declaration of Human Rights
1949	UN brokers peace between Israel and Arabs
1950	Security Council agrees on UN intervention in aid of South Korea
	Beginning of Korean War (to 1953)
	UNICEF set up
1953	Dag Hammarskjöld becomes secretary-general
1955	Sixteen new member states accepted
1956	General Assembly sets up first UN peacekeeping force for Suez
1959	UN organizes treaty banning **nuclear weapons** from Antarctica
1960	UN troops sent to Congo
1961	U Thant becomes secretary-general
1962	World Food Program established
1964	UN force sent to Cyprus
1965	Security Council membership rises to 15
1969	UN Fund for Population Activities set up
1971	People's Republic of China replaces Taiwan as China's UN representative
1972	Kurt Waldheim becomes secretary-general
1973	UN force sent to Middle East
1974	UN Special Committee Against Apartheid established
1978	UN force sent to Lebanon
1982	Javier Pérez de Cuéllar becomes secretary-general
1983	World Commission on Environment and Development founded
1984	United States leaves UNESCO
1987	Montreal Protocol on phasing out gases that damage the Earth's ozone layer
1988	UN forces sent to Afghanistan, Pakistan, Iran, and Iraq

1990	Iraq invades Kuwait: UN-approved coalition against Iraq: Gulf War (to 1991)
1992	Boutros Boutros-Ghali becomes secretary-general
	Earth Summit in Rio de Janeiro
	UN force enters former Yugoslavia
	UN force sent to Cambodia
1993	UN missions take place in Uganda, Rwanda, Georgia, and Haiti
1995	UN Conference on Women, held in Beijing, China
1997	Kofi Annan becomes secretary-general
	Widespread reform of UN started
	Kyoto Protocol on global warming drawn up
1998	UN enforcement troops sent to East Timor
2001	Terrorist attack New York and Washington, D.C.
	UN backs U.S. "war on terrorism"

Further Reading

Isaacs, Sally Senzell. *America in the Time of Franklin Delano Roosevelt: The Story of Our Nation from Coast to Coast, from 1929 to 1948.* Chicago: Heinemann Library, 1999.

Maass, Robert. *UN Ambassador: A Behind-the-Scenes Look at Madeleine Albright's World.* Collindale, Pa.: Diane Publishing Company, 2000.

Melvern, Linda. *United Nations.* Danbury, Conn.: Franklin Watts, 2001.

Powell, Jillian. *The World Health Organization.* Danbury, Conn.: Franklin Watts, 2001.

Prior, Katherine. *UNICEF.* Danbury, Conn.: Franklin Watts, 2001.

Tubbs, April. *Understanding the United Nations.* Minneapolis, Minn.: United Nations Association of Minnesota, 1999.

Taylor, David. *The Cold War.* Chicago: Heinemann Library, 2001.

Glossary

Allied powers countries (including the United Kingdom, France, the United States, and the USSR) that fought together against Germany, Italy, and Japan during World War II (1939–45)

annexed taken over by a neighboring territory, often without consultation

arbitration process of judging a case by an arbitrator

arbitrator someone accepted by groups in dispute to make a judgment in their case

boycott to refuse to have dealings with an organization or nation

British Commonwealth association (founded in 1931) of the United Kingdom and some formerly British-controlled territories. In 1945, its members were the United Kingdom, Australia, Canada, Irish Free State, Newfoundland, New Zealand, and South Africa.

capitalist based on an economic system in which land, factories, and other ways of producing goods are owned and controlled by individuals, not the government

CNN Cable News Network, a U.S.-based news and media organization

coercive using force

colony territory governed by another country

communist someone who follows communism, a political movement that aims to create a classless society in which the means of production are owned in common

convention agreement between states

corruption dishonest behavior by people in public office

crimes against humanity wrongs committed against a whole population or parts of a population

democratic conforming to the principles of rule by the people, in which a government is run by representatives who are elected by the public

dictator ruler with absolute authority

disarmament giving up of or a reduction in armed forces or weapons

economic sanctions measures taken to prevent trade with a particular country

epidemic disease that is passed among large numbers of people

free trade economic system that allows people to trade with as little government interference or control as possible

genocide killing of a large number of people

human rights conditions deserved by all human beings, such as freedom, equality, or justice

humanitarian promoting the well-being and social rights of humans

infantry division large military unit of soldiers trained to fight on foot

International Monetary Fund international organization of 183 member countries founded in 1946 to establish monetary cooperation and stability, promote economic growth and employment, and provide temporary financial assistance to individual countries

left-wing pursuing political change to gain greater freedom for ordinary people

mediate help sort out differences

nationalization making an industry the property of a nation

Nazi member of the German National Socialist Workers' Party, a racist, violent, and antidemocratic political group that ruled Germany from 1933–45

nuclear weapons weapons whose destructive power comes from an uncontrolled nuclear reaction

ozone gas that forms a layer in the earth's upper atmosphere, blocking most of the Sun's ultraviolet radiation

pacific rejecting the use of force

People's Republic of China name of the communist state of mainland China since 1949

proliferation rapid increase in numbers

protocol records of what was said and agreed upon at a conference

radical person who desires extreme political or social changes

refugee person who flees from his or her country to another

republic country in which power rests with the people and their elected representatives

right-wing favoring strong government and opposing changes to the traditional social order

Russian Federation country formed in 1991 from the remains of the USSR after Ukraine, Belarus, Moldova, and the Soviet republics in central Asia and the Baltic became independent

superpower major world power, usually referring to the United States and the USSR, 1945–91

sustainable development using resources without depleting or damaging them

Third World developing nations of the world

treaty negotiated agreement between countries

tribunal type of law court

unanimous having the consent of all parties

USSR Union of Soviet Socialist Republics; until its collapse in 1990, a communist superpower dominated by Russia

veto power to prohibit action by others

weapons of mass destruction weapons, such as nuclear or chemical weapons, that can kill entire populations

West noncommunist countries of Europe and the United States

Western term describing the democratic nations of North America and Western Europe

World Bank UN organization established to assist world economic development primarily through loans

Index